Pebble® Plus

How to Build
Flipsticks

Hands-On SCIENCE FUN

by Lori Shores

Consulting Editor: Gail Saunders-Smith, PhD

Consultant: Ronald Browne, PhD
Department of Elementary & Early Childhood Education
Minnesota State University, Mankato

CAPSTONE PRESS
a capstone imprint

Pebble Plus is published by Capstone Press,
1710 Roe Crest Drive, North Mankato, Minnesota 56003.
www.capstonepub.com

Library of Congress Cataloging-in-Publication Data
Shores, Lori.
  How to build flipsticks / by Lori Shores.
    p. cm.—(Pebble plus. Hands-on science fun)
  Summary: "Simple text and full-color photos instruct readers how to build flipsticks and explain the science behind
the activity"—Provided by publisher.
  Includes bibliographical references and index.
  ISBN 978-1-4296-5292-6 (library binding)
  ISBN 978-1-4296-6213-0 (paperback)
  1. Motion perception (Vision)—Juvenile literature. 2. Flipsticks (Toy)—Experiments—Juvenile literature. 3.
Science—Study and teaching (Preschool)—Activity programs—Juvenile literature. 4. Science—Study and teaching
(Primary)—Activity programs—Juvenile literature. I. Title. II. Series.
  QP493.S56 2011
  612.8'4—dc22
                                                                          2010024908

Editorial Credits
Erika L. Shores, editor; Gene Bentdahl, designer; Sarah Schuette, photo shoot direction; Marcy Morin, scheduler;
    Laura Manthe, production specialist

Photo Credits
All photos by Capstone Studio/Karon Dubke, except page 17 (brain illustration), Shutterstock/Oguz Aral

Note to Parents and Teachers

The Hands-On Science Fun series supports national science standards related to physical
science. This book describes and illustrates how to build a flipstick. The images support early
readers in understanding the text. The repetition of words and phrases helps early readers
learn new words. This book also introduces early readers to subject-specific vocabulary words,
which are defined in the Glossary section. Early readers may need assistance to read some
words and to use the Table of Contents, Glossary, Read More, Internet Sites, and Index sections
of the book.

Printed in China.
062014
008330R

Table of Contents

Safety Note:
Please ask an adult for help in building your flipstick.

Getting Started

What does this project have
to do with your favorite cartoon?
They both trick your brain
into seeing pictures move!

Here's what you need:

white paper

2 index cards

pencil

scissors

markers

tape

5

Making a Flipstick

Trace an index card

twice on white paper.

Cut out the boxes.

On one piece, draw an alien

with arms at its sides.

On the other piece of paper,

trace the alien except

for the arms.

Draw the alien's arms lifted up.

Use markers to color
the drawings.

Tape the drawings
to the index cards.

Tape the end of the pencil
to the back of one card.

Tape the cards together
with the pencil between them.

Hold the pencil between your palms.

Rub your hands together to spin the pencil.

What happens?

How Does It Work?

When you look at
a picture, your eyes send
a message to your brain.
When the picture is removed,
your brain remembers it.

When you see two drawings
quickly, your brain blends
the pictures together.
The two pictures look like
one moving image.

Animated cartoons are made up of many pictures. Each picture is shown for only part of a second. We see the pictures as moving cartoons.

Glossary

alien—a creature from another planet

animated cartoon—a series of drawings shown very quickly so that they appear to move

project—an assignment that is worked on over a period of time

trace—to copy a picture or shape by following lines seen through a piece of thin paper